MORE OF ME DISAPPEARS

To Craig —

Thanks so much!

All my best,

[signature]

02/07/06

ALSO BY JOHN AMEN

POETRY

Christening the Dancer (2003)

MUSIC

All I'll Never Need (2004)

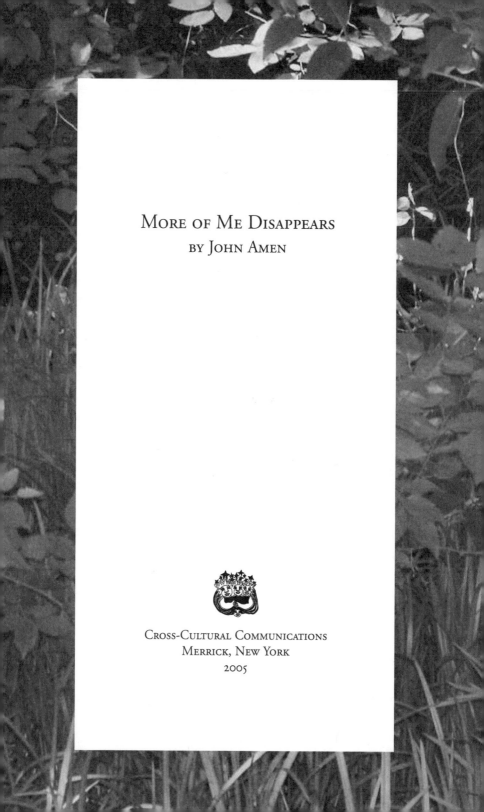

More of Me Disappears
by John Amen

Cross-Cultural Communications
Merrick, New York
2005

ISBN 0-89304-888-7

Editor-Publisher: Stanley H. Barkan

CROSS-CULTURAL COMMUNICATIONS
239 Wynsum Avenue
Merrick, NY 11566-4725 / USA
Tel: 516.868.5636 Fax: 516.379.1901
cccpoetry@aol.com
cross-culturalcommunications.com

First Edition

Book Cover and Book Design:
Mary Kerr Powers / symbioticdesign.biz

Photography: John Amen

Published in the United States of America

"It's sweet to have all this nonsense, noise ..."
—Tu Fu

I

II

III

I

THE CONSUMMATION
for Mary

i

Without warning,
the river runs dry, its spine
as glutted and songless as any morgue.

Worms petrify on their hajj
toward the center of the earth.
The cactus, spoiled child,
mocks its heavy-eyed companions.

ii

I swallow dust until my petition for rain
penetrates a bureaucracy of sky.

I voice words of affinity and umbrage:
I want you to know that I am here, invested,
craving you as shadow craves substance.

Still, water remains the prodigal son.
Grass, concubine to the dewdrop,
mumbles its still-umber protest,
my garden as bloody as a slaughtered lamb.

iii

So many voices in the vestibule of anger;
Noah's beasts go mad in their cages. A cipher
is upon me; in this garden of wilted grace,
I search for *agape* as if it were an Easter egg.

iv

The creek learns to walk again, shuffles
tentatively through bones of pine and oak.

I am perusing old calendars, love letters,
diaries from my spring of darkness:

There *were* days when a diva sang,
when roses bloomed like jazz.
I recall the sky red with intention.
The pimpled face in the mirror
was not always that of an enemy.

v

Summer arrives like a parole hearing.
Starlings banter in the charcoal night.

In my imaginings, I am broken
by storms as violent as a mother's tongue.
In truth, I endure, persisting like a desert,
immune to tomorrow's taunting.

Like energy, you and I cannot be destroyed.
We are made of holy water and the feces of a god.
How does it feel to be immortal?

LAST WORDS

Cut loose from the womb of my ship,
drifting like Icarus in this white suit,

destiny is broken down to numbers,
x amount of inhalations, x temperature

tolerable, knowing that a breathless
demise is what awaits me. You tickle

my ear like an insect, urgent whispers
wrapped in static; dissecting my silence

as if I were the first person to enter
the house of God. There is no gauging

my location now. This is true transcendence,
mind meeting the unknown, language

unavailable, the brain itself groping for
impulses to send south to the body. This is

what I wanted, to die in the mouth of the sun,
lungs imploding like a flattened can, all sense

of mortal obligation cauterized like a wound.
A moment can indeed define a lifetime,

karma be vaporized at the threshold of death.
Light floods like a big bang; kiss the earth

for yours truly; tell the paparazzi I went home,
energy forever burning in the belly of the mother star.

IN THE MAKING

I wake to see my story convulsing beside me.
Someone has stuck a fork in the moon's eye.

I underline passages I cannot read,
wander like an anorexic from mirror to mirror.

The sky opens like an earring clasp.
Angels scream safe words,
but the great domina is deaf.

The irises are made of plastic.
Soothe, please, my brain's cauliflower ears.

Sirens sing, but no one speaks their language.

My name is a boa. I am the canary writhing in its throat.

VERBOTEN

We are in Paris, my grandparents and I,
visiting my grandfather's sister, the one who
failed to get out of Europe in 1938. I am
seven years old. My great-aunt's arms remind
me of spaghetti strands, and she speaks
in a high, labored voice, as if a little
pump inside her is not working right.
They are drinking wine and speaking
of French-U.S. relations when the long
sleeve on her arm falls down. Before
she can clutch it, I see the faded blue
tattoo on her flesh. "What are those
numbers?" I ask. A silence explodes
through the room like spores.
My aunt picks up a tray of empty
glasses and retreats into the kitchen.
"Some questions," my grandfather
says, rubbing his own unblemished arm,
"should not be asked." As life went on,
I learned that most of the questions
I wanted answers to fell into that category.
Still, I asked them; and I'm still asking them.

MEANWHILE
—Sangerberg, 1945

At the courthouse, a tailor was
being sentenced. It was raining tofu.
The hibiscus, like a snail, slept
inside its folded bloom. Sidewalks
groaned beneath bassinets, mothers
baring their breasts at prayer hour.

Someone cut down the hanging tree.
Somebody's son fondled a trigger.
The operation was a success.
Geese were trapped in the funeral tent,
wings burning like chandeliers.

A few days later, a clown emerged
from a darkroom, his throat on fire
for the first time. Odd things commenced.
No one believed that water flowed uphill.
The sun did not rise. Gravity lifted like an embargo.
We glued ourselves together, marched on.

THINGS ARE HAPPENING TOO FAST

The wings of the world
are flapping like a fish in a dry pail.

Sometimes I terrify myself,
the things I could destroy.

There is a rainbow above the refinery;
in the hammock of stars, a scribe is weeping.

I pass like a current
through empty sockets of my mother's skull.

The day emerges like a mole.

Our Father, deaf and mute in the gilded air.

P.S. FROM PARADISE

The mint is on fire, green smog hovering
over the playground. The Pope is about to
announce a winner. The President dances
on a half-lit floor surrounded by Secret
Service men. My roof leaks. Pyramids
of thought become anthills in a killing field.
The doors of the elevator will not close.
A gay couple marries at the bottom of the ocean.
After a trinity of bombs and Augustine's
filibuster, all debts are forgiven. The Rapture
is finally proclaimed an American holiday.
Sleep well, cosmos; better luck next time.

ANGELICA TELLS HER STORY

"True, human beings are strange ..."
—Rainer Maria Rilke, "The Voices"

I used to ride a bus to the suburbs, visit
my insane sister in her white prison, floors lined
with withered petals, pages from her bloody diary.
On days of armistice and amnesty,
I would have my palm read by a bald gypsy.
Sometimes soldiers showered me with gewgaws.
My mother was a mannequin with red eyes.
I watched the earth swallow my father limb by limb.
I remember my old town as you remember an eccentric aunt;
snapshots emerge from thorny darkness;
words and incidents wash over me like hunger.
Oh Marta, I suffered until laughter crawled
up the birth canal of my heart and cried its lungs awake.
I grieve for my sister, still chained to the storm in her gray pulp;
my mother, who died looking out a window; my father,
who left behind account books, a car we sold on the internet.
Paradox is my native tongue. Oh Marta, when late April dawns,
when snows melt and spring is finally suckled, I want to remember
where I come from. If I forget, please, will you remind me?

IN A REVOLVING DOOR

I am in Neverland buying gifts for my geisha girl
when I hear the news—war has broken out.
We hit the dance club as death reports surface.
Mars is a fallout shelter. Skies above Venus
are blacker than a presidential limo. Economies sag
like laundry lines. Someone tries to steal my wallet.
I call my geisha girl on the telewave. Her blue heart
is as pure as cash. She asks me when I am coming home.
"There's no telling," I say. "Intergalactics have started
destroying the transporters." –"OK," she mumbles,
"I'll put on the coffee." Routine is all, routine is God.

THE LEGACY
for Rochelle

So far, the reach of terror—
steel fingers clawing in sand,
a missile's wake wagging
through gray skies
like a burning tail.

The ivory man is speaking,
words rolling like tanks
through a dreamscape of bridges
toward oil fields, fertile mesas
where grief is the native tongue.

We are in this madness together,
feasting at a smorgasbord of hunger,
faces buried in the lap of death.
So soon silence falls,
a mother's nightmare.

The drama ceases to be real,
the imagination disappointed.
Barrages and sorties occur
between meals
as the trash is being taken out.

The epic is the shadow of the commonplace,
an empty gale after pollen has settled.
Our secret fears
manifest without fanfare
precisely as we clench the deal.

Roads are potholed, littered with skulls
of a past generation's ambition,
Adam's fractured rage
impaled on a spear, left
for broadcasters to interpret.

INSTANT MESSAGE FROM A BIGWIG

I'm playing checkers with a rabbi
while his messenger massages my feet.
The Ark has sprung a leak again.
Zebras are eating the magnolia blooms.

I was supposed to be in London
four days ago, but the mist swelled
like a snake bite, and now I'm stranded
outside this convoy of trailers, this crescent
of all-you-can-eat restaurants. Heat
pounds like a railway tie. Nothing gives.

The rabbi orders a container of turpentine
and blesses his messenger, who leaves
on a bicycle with a flat tire. A woman
late for bingo drives recklessly, hits him
head-on three minutes and forty-one seconds
later. The idiot savant predicts a famine, though
no one hears him, absorbed in wedding plans.

By the time I reach dream number one million,
I will have become God. Chased the equinox
barefoot through snow. Collected wheat
during a frog-storm. Signed Judas's petition.
Already something else is ending.

SO MANY LIVES
for Ed

At six, I'd fall out of bed, the white poison still
clinging to my veins, the drug's sultry voice
echoing in my head. Jim had a job at a Wal-Mart
across town, and Lisa was a dancer at a men's club
on Old Pineville. The three of us needed somewhere
to stay and we figured if we chipped in together we
might be able to get a decent place. I'd make the meetings
every evening, tumbling out of some Samaritan's car
with my coffee mug and packs of cigarettes. I spent
mornings filling out applications. My sponsor had me
leading a prison meeting on Tuesday afternoons in Lincolnton.
But I'll never forget coming home that Thursday night–
finding the place trashed, as if a wild animal had been
rummaging for food, Jim sprawled in a pile of beer bottles,
a used syringe in his hand. I tried to revive him, but he was
already cold, his lips a pale blue, like the cotton candy I
used to get at the circus when I was a kid. Paramedics and police
converged: *How did he get it? Who did he get it from?*
Where were you when this happened? Did you know he had it?
The next day Lisa moved out. I left a couple of weeks later.
I was ninety days sober, and everything and nothing seemed possible.
I got a job at a warehouse, driving forklifts all day. I only ran
into Lisa once after that, but years later I saw her in a grocery store
carrying a bottle of wine toward the checkout counter. I was
with my wife, who could see that the expression on my face
had changed, and she asked me if I knew that woman, and by then Lisa
had paid and left the store, and I didn't feel like going into details, so
I just mumbled, *Yeah, she looks familiar. I think I know her from meetings.*
But then some voice kicked in and told me I couldn't afford to keep secrets,
especially from my wife, and we went and had coffee at the shop next door,
and I told her everything, the entire story. And now I've told you, too.

REMAINS

Epic themes have become cliché: Oedipus,
Hercules, Odysseus, the long-standing classical

brainwash. The macro and micro have come apart
like Siamese twins freed by the knife. God knows

where each has set up shop. I'm not sure that strings
run down from the heavens any longer, that Campbell's

dearly beloved myths still spiral on our street corners.
Sometimes it seems that they, like the birds

of summer, have flown toward balmier regions,
that what we have left here is empty space and

what we fill it with—nothing more, nothing less.

A SMALL SPACE

After rubbing stardust from my eyes,
I witness the storm holding its breath.

I realize how much I love the things that hurt me.

Even the weather vane pauses before pointing
toward the country where I was born.

Theories, antonyms keep me busy
while angels sign the cast of my humor.

If love is a horse, good luck saddling it.

THE VOID
for Tom

I stand alone in this cipher-house,
casting spells, the destroyer upon me.
My scarecrows are ruptured like piñatas.

The mad race to fill the empty room begins;
I turn defeats into stained glass, shatter
crucifixion scenes, offer shards to rapacious women,
who dice me into canapés. My serenades are
little more than ice cubes in their before-dinner drinks.

I search for a map and find a blank canvas.
I want salvation but end up with the poison
ivy of hollow hours. My rash, your rash, is invisible.

THE ASCENT

i

Vagrants are clawing at the car door.
A madman beats his oars against the water.

Now we are called to rummage.

This morning, I saw
the invisible child, a gavel in his pocket.

I do not need people to empathize with this.

I marched through burning asphalt toward my mother;
I was erect, and I did not feel like dying.

Here is a soundproofed room,
and here are your screams. You should know
by now, the singular is always a tragedy.

ii

Teeth marks on the azalea blossoms.
Lightning has struck the sycamore twice now.

Congratulations, we are in the throat of things:

There are random swaths in the grass.
The sky spirals like a coat of arms.

Give me back some of what has been taken.

The carnations are drunk again.

The fire in the kitchen was never extinguished.

iii

What twists in the grass, what writhes
in the bedroom, is the memory unretrieved.

Gravel in the driveway thinned like hair.

Give me my moment of fullness.
My memorials have stood long enough.

The wound in my groin is healed.

By the time the teeth of night grind,
I will remember that I am indeed blessed.

BREATHING

i

Nowadays things unravel
between armloads of stone,
trips to the river of convenience;
I find myself in thick patches of thistle,
running barefoot through acres of hemlock.

Evening falls like confetti;
darkness is the coda in this symphony of habit.

I'm not sure that my eyes will last this lifetime.
What if my voice cracks during the song's crescendo?

ii

Someday, when fools channel lightning,
when dogwood blossoms line courthouse steps,
you and I will carve heirlooms for your children.

I will memorize your family tree, run
hands through broken cogs and algae as gods
implode like a vampire exposed to the sun.

Our alphabet will be formed from configurations of ash,
scales from the cries of a wounded merman.
Already lovers line the riverbanks.

The crepe myrtle twists like a ballerina.
A dictator's speech echoes in our bedroom;
fields of pachysandra and periwinkle burn.

iii

What tower of Babel crashes to the barren ground now?
What hairless Samson loiters in the rubble of his own making?

Thousands of faces beneath veils. A child roaming
corridors looking for his parents' bedroom. Fire
awakens like a beast, nuzzling white walls, raping curtains,
devouring rooms like a boa swallowing a rodent.

Brutus, Iago, Judas, the Land of Nod with its boundaries
of bone, sin, and blood. Shrinking rooms of the brain,
dark chambers roped off. Screams in the dungeon.

Buy familiar images in the gift shop of teeth.
Buy souvenirs, posters, memorabilia of phlegm.

What has changed since dawn?
Has the cactus finally died of thirst?
I hear hoarse voices swelling like a blister.

iv

When spring's fullness rages like a master's palette,
when you grow heavy with remembrance, I promise
to strum my guitar until your muse descends,
the perfect lyrics and melody deliver you.

I am ready, like birds after rain.
I promise to water the geraniums.
I promise to sharpen the knives.
I promise to take measurements.

I promise to sing while the termite gnaws.

V

My shoes are on fire with my own persistent story;
my throat is raw, and the things I wish to forget
continue to stalk me. Moods change like fashion;
these days anything can be reupholstered.

A crowd is screaming; waters part.
The dream is being interpreted:
feast and famine are Siamese twins.

When doubt lingers like an infection,
I will balance our books, finalize plans,
paint a rainbow with semen and feces.
We are going to need electricity and steel, all the
thick mud of Eden, beneath scabs of forgiveness.

NEW YORK MEMORY #3

When I get to my dead father's apartment,
Liz emerges from ruptured planks and exploded plaster.
She is covered with soot, like some pagan baptized
in refuse. The wrecking crew has come before
we had a chance to vacate the place, stripped the loft
to its skeleton. My father's furniture has been destroyed,
a lifetime buried beneath an avalanche of wood and iron.
Beds have been gutted, paintings raped by protruding nails.
A fast-food cup rises from the ruin like a conqueror's flag.
The apartment is quickly remodeled, rent raised;
the revolving door of humanity spins. Over the years,
I make a point of knowing who is living there. I see tenants
come and go. I accept that we're not so unlike animals.
I mean, I have this friend who tells me all about bees,
how the queen is revered and protected, ultimately
replaced in a savage deposition, how the mad
hive continues, greater than any one member.
And everything he says sounds familiar, and stings.

EULOGY FOR MY MOTHER

My mother was a young swallow
abandoned to my care. I raised her to adulthood
and set her free. I see her occasionally now,
mostly at sunset when clouds pass like wild geese.

I call her by her christened name.
On summer evenings, she builds nests
in the awnings of my house,
splashes in birdbaths in my backyard.

Sometimes she stares through the window,
but never with longing. I have become God,
and she is Cain, who slew Abel, my child-self.
I tell her to wander, but I put a mark

on her feathery brow, that she might not
perish at the hands of other blind mothers.
She thanks me for it, for severing that cord;
in songs as piercing as evening rain,
grieves she was unable to cut it herself.

KARMA

We were waiting for the moon to appear, arpeggios soaring from my instrument, fingers, bow. By the time Christ made his appearance, you were on the verge of orgasm. "Love thy neighbor," he said, and you screamed in his ear as your hips lurched like a racecar. I reached crescendo as he displayed his palms for the world to see. "Do you deny me now?" he asked. You blew smoke rings as wine gushed from his wounds. I cleaned my cello and prepared to rehearse the scene again.

PLAYBOY

I pass through a turnstile, find myself playing scrabble with the dog catcher. "I've got to find my friends," I say. "I think something terrible is scheduled for sunset." He dashes the scrabble board to the ground. Darkness is swimming into the day, eating it in small, methodical bites. I am at the end of the compound when the spotlights flash on. "Surprise," my friends bellow, their fangs emerging beneath false moonlight. Then they take me on their shoulders and begin singing "God Bless America."

FADE

My mother is sleeping in a crib lined with barbed wire; water rises from the floorboards. Upstairs the accountant is arguing with a rabbi. The news is on. My father reclines in our electric chair, polishing his horns as he sings the multiplication tables. My mother can neither fray her flesh nor bleed. She gorges on communion wafers stolen from the revival. "Who do you think you are," she yells at the ceiling, "Apollo?" I begin flipping through the yellow pages, looking for an exorcist willing to make a house call.

AT FIRST

Celebrities gathered beside the pool, drinking champagne, gorging themselves on raw beef. You stood at the top of the stairs like a heroine in a B-movie. I watched you as the piano moaned under my fingers. "Is this an audition?" I yelled. The celebrities wept in unison. "*Namaste*," they chanted. I could have composed a hundred sonatas with a single flourish. I looked to the top of the stairs again. You were gone, your white dress drooped across the banister, a trace of you shimmering in the fluorescent light. It would be lifetimes before I would see you again.

FIVE

My mother is stammering in a language I have yet to learn, tumors gnawing through her pink flesh; my father has passed out, eyes glued shut with gin and hard barbiturates. I pound on his granite body until my fists are purple. My mother is on her knees like a supplicant, lost in her coda of dying, as my father's snores crescendo. Then, silence, darkness. When the image returns, as if someone has performed a splice, my mother's body is covered with a sheet and my father is asking a paramedic for a cigarette. I've been trying for years to find that missing piece of film, but these canisters of memory are empty, and the search just goes on and on and on.

IN A DAY'S JOURNEY

i

After the war, my Siamese twin and I wander the rugged mesa,
navigating corpses as if they were landmines.

There are engine parts scattered in the palmetto; oil and steel
gleam in the noon sun.

My twin, he is like Milton's God, beyond remorse. I am the one
wearing the chastity belt, a company watch, my mother's maiden
name, tattooed on my scrotum in 1971.

"The dark man has died for us," my twin says as a maggot sips
blood from his flip-flop. The sky couldn't be bluer.

ii

The fallout shelter is garish. Video monitors are broken, curtains
tattered like old wigs.

I enter my cheap cubicle, still sporting a bulletproof vest;
the sorcerer leaps from a closet, dressed in overalls,
his hair dyed blue; he grabs my throat as if it were a banister,
jams a plastic tube into my mouth.

"Drink the world," he tells me. "Swallow!" Pegasus is floating in
the neon air outside the stockade.

iii

I've turned my tenement into an evangelical tourist site.
Strangers flock daily to see my cracked symbols, worn walkways,
beads of sweat clinging to glass.

They are drawn to my Tower of Babel. "Is it true," they ask, "up there you can see the genitals of God?"

I point to the trepanned hole in my left temple. "*This*," I stutter, "is where the tour begins."

They follow me, riding escalators into humid darkness; there we will encounter orphans, men who fuck roasted chickens, ghosts in shawls of water.

iv

I earned my certificate and have returned to inspect the nursery, floor littered with pacifiers and yo-yos.

The nanny cannot find her prosthetic leg.
She will not give me a cigarette.

The cribs are empty, hatches open. Cold air burps into the room.
There are fingerprints on the glass, footprints in the garden,
mammoth soles disappearing into the test zone.

I call this angel I met at a hot dog stand.
Her cell phone rings and rings.
Somehow I couldn't care less how things turn out,
whether I make it home by morning.

NEW YORK MEMORY #10

Every month, when her body revolted with that
wild urge to breed, we would take a yellow cab
to an upper east side fertility clinic. The waiting
room was filled with bellicose women, shell-shocked
men twitching in their seats. Doctors and nurses
probed with gloved hands, inserted my masturbated seed
into her pummeled orifice. We felt as if we were in a casino,
the way they always said "good luck" before we left.
And then, a few days later, we'd return, having
fucked like robots, and they'd run their tests. We'd leave
again, find some diner or Italian joint to eat at, before
ending up back at the brownstone. And then around five,
they'd call. "I'm sorry," they'd tell her, "you're not pregnant."
They said that for four or five months, and I hate to admit it,
but every time, a huge part of me was relieved.

AMBIVALENCE

Darkness and dawn wrestled in the alley.
The yucca bloomed as bridges collapsed.

The singer had forgotten his lyrics;
rain was flooding from an electric sky.

Summer faded like a tattoo.
Reluctance exploded like ballet.

Everywhere I looked I saw torn bibles,
hymnals scattered in a gutter. The sun
sank into the ocean like a burning anchor.

When I came to, I was holding a shotgun.

BEFORE ANYTHING SETTLES

My beautiful dread is draped
across April's new sculpture.

I daydream in a rotting cradle.

There is rust on the gate.
Remonstrance returns like heartburn.

The altar of atoms looms.

Sometimes I think I have lost myself
in phonebooks and metal shavings.

After darkness is sealed like a mason jar,
I ask the stars if they care to learn my name.

PERSISTENCE

This morning I slept in ambition's arms,
dreamt of my mother climbing a stairwell.

I am equal parts water, ash, and illusion.

The sky belched stars as the earth meditated.

I am committed to nonsense, as well.

What I believe is a cracked conch
echoing in my ear. God bless the mad.

There is a gift being offered.

I am chiseling through ice to receive it.

NOTICE

I'm going on sabbatical for a bit,
so fill my space with whatever
you choose. The moon is bulging
like a boil; the earth is winding down.
I suppose I should get back to you
in the morning, after I've had a chance
to sleep on it. But I have to say, I'm
not so sure about some of this anymore.
Tomorrow I'm canceling the newspaper.
I may not retrieve the mail for a spell.
Forgive me if I don't answer the phone.
I'll be back, but probably not in time
to witness the next round of sex and death.

WHAT I SAID TO MYSELF

Choose the butterfly over the chrysalis.
Choose light, the ballroom, the well-lit restaurant.

You have for lifetimes strummed minor chords
on the coast of a dead sea. Think major, spindrift.

The sex between you and grief is becoming mechanical.

Despite your vestigial sentiments to the contrary,
a scab's story is much greater than that of a scar.

Your cock is not an umbilical cord, it is your
heart's mouthpiece. Choose sunrise, please.

It is time to do something that might cause
embarrassment. Let emptiness mother your child.

Put away the map, where we're going won't be on it.

There is nothing particularly inspiring about a death wish.

You have learned all there is to learn from the woman in black.

It is time to stop insulting ecstasy. Masochism
is an empty udder. What was is a cipher. Pick
the rose over the injured dove. Pick warm waters.

Attend a circus. Go for the comic. There is nothing
more mediocre than the association of dysfunction with genius.

Indulge in color. Believe me, there is not a problem.
Plumb bright places for new symbols.

Recommendation: study evergreens.
Find me. We have much to talk about.

III

VACILLATIONS

"Tonight as always
There is no one to share my thoughts."
        —Chu Shu Chen

1.

The sky stretches like a yogi;
yesterday was a nightmare that would not end;

today, that is forgotten;
butterflies christen my gables.

I am a creature of habit; then again,
there is no predicting what I will sing tomorrow.

2.

Dogwood blossoms throb in the twilight,
whispering in a code I cannot decipher.

Cicadas swarm like tourists; frogs
conspire behind every blade of grass.

The beauty of these days is unbearable.
August again—sleep feels like suicide.

3.

Words stick to my brain like burrs. I am
bearing the twins of meaning and bondage.

The arsonist strikes a match; the .38 backfires.
A Rottweiler is baying outside the prison.

My secrets are as common as dull razors.
It is true, this cliché about attachment and misery.

4.

Irritation thrashes in my gut.
Paramedics are smoking in the backyard.

There is more than one Mecca, one Medina.
I will be like pollen, settling in distant places.

The day is my field; love is made of wind.
What shall we harvest tomorrow?

5.

My liver clutches grief.
Children sharpen knives in the driveway.

There is a witch chanting in my pancreas.
"Have you crafted a saddle for your mind?"

the guru asks me, and a memory begins
to surface, like mutant worms after a bombing.

6.

We always end up in a strange town
staring into a kaleidoscope, discussing

the ash and ember of our days. A man is
playing a familiar song on a stolen guitar.

We cross many bridges, sleep in monasteries.
Seasons come and go; lifetimes, too.

7.

The music of the iris is hard to withstand;
its purple song claws at my heart;

its sister, the azalea, is incoherent, slurring;
the dogwood, plaintive brother, sips a whiskey of moonlight.

Forsythia, monomaniacal cousin, tosses its yellow garb
on the walkway; grass recites fairytales to the patient oak.

8.

Blue of the birdbath, lilies like a plea,
sky yawning: the riddles of my life in abeyance.

Could I ask for more? Water is abundant. I have
written three songs today. The squall arrived

and passed like a poker player's bluff. Tonight
will be what it is: I am a child in an amusement park.

9.

The sun bleeds into the ocean, dying
a slow death. The lighthouse trembles.

Dogs are growling by the fence. Long hours
settle like a mattress; the sky clears its throat.

Stars rise like a man doing a push-up. I sit
cross-legged in the sand, drum until rainy dawn.

10.

I cannot put my finger on what
is stomping up and down my spine.

Shadows spread like an oil spill.
Summer approaches like a tribe of cannibals.

I will stumble into my greatest creation.
There is so much left to translate.

11.

Cardinals are singing in lime-green trees;
the sun is fading like a child abducted by a stranger.

I cannot make the necessary phone calls this evening;
I can only watch the wind rub its palm across the lake.

The swollen gardenia is crying; the serpent has
bitten the dove. Doubt avalanches like a truckload of coal.

12.

A hurricane has torn through my paperwork.
Suspicions are disappearing like a head cold.

The maples are as full as sex. Thick hedges,
bird nests, owls yodeling in the afternoon.

The garden takes shape like a maturing girl.
Soon there will be fireflies flickering over the lawn.

13.

Love is rising like bread. I stared
into the eyes of thirteen specific demons;

I rewrote my birth date. In a fog
as thick as algebra, new information came to me.

I have no use for tenses now. All the world
is a puddle, and I am a boy in a new pair of boots.

14.

I am grateful for all the green in our veins.
Ivy wraps around gravestones. Lyrics flow

like lamb's blood. Leaves are quaking on the branch.
Each day more of me disappears.

I have no need to doctor the withered fig tree.
The wheat is full, and crickets revel outside my window.

IN A GIVEN MOMENT

What I can tell you is
dead skin will fall from us soon.

The wheel spins backwards.

Sometimes
I feel I can ventriloquize no longer.

Even the dry bones
in my pocket grow new flesh.

The dice will not stop tumbling.

Morning is here again. It
has carried its secret a long way.

NARCISSISM

Every night, from closing time until
morning's drugged-out yawn, I'd
comb the 24-hour diners looking
for my heroin-damsel, glaring
into the eyes of pimps and escorts
counting their green in shadowy booths.

I'd find her in forsaken Bronx neighborhoods,
ramshackle Brooklyn brownstones,
her ebony skin pitted pink by the needle,
drool trickling down her bruised neck, battered limbs.
Like Gabriel himself, I'd whisk her home
amidst a storm of accusations. She'd sleep
like a vampire long past noon's impatient stare.

A few months later, when she got clean,
I realized I missed those desultory nights,
pumping adrenaline, the sirens of crisis,
how alive I felt with a barrel pressed
against my temple. She left me for a
Cuban evangelist with a day-time talk show.
They moved to Los Angeles and wooed a loyal flock.

I took on a litany of candidates, women
who begged me to save them and cursed
the marrow in my bones. I finally crashed
in a clinic outside Baton Rouge, spent
six months in a white suit, staring at my
broken love line. It's strange how lifetimes
have flowed like water in a bong, how I still
curse the hungry stillness, this agonizing calm,
what seems like the sleep of atoms,
the universe itself droopy-eyed and comatic.

What happened to those days
when God seemed like my personal dispatcher,
when I'd make rounds, fixing lives like a master repairman?
What happened to the possessed and dying?
Was I forsaken for some other right-hand man,
some amateur Iago who caressed the great boss's ego
precisely when his divine doubt
swarmed like sickness before the fix?

ONE NIGHT IN ARIZONA

The moon looks on, amused voyeur.
A mother sits by the birdcage

darning socks for the young priest.
Heat hangs over the house like a quilt.

We have not spoken for months,
key broken off in a lock of silence.

The desert stretches like a gauntlet,
nothing between me and the dust

but this thin membrane: distraction.

NEW YORK MEMORY #14

It wasn't so bad, that November, that sad month,
bleakness settling into the New York landscape.
Wind came off the East River, carrying dank secrets,
tickling the manes of gargoyles, slicing through
layers of clothing. I didn't write those days, took up art,
large canvases, big, loose strokes with acrylic paint.
I walked down Court Street in the evenings, sat on
the Promenade sometimes. My father was dead;
we were just married, and I wasn't happy, but
maybe things seemed all right. We were eating
fattening food, not arguing too much. In a department
store near St Mark's, we decided to have a baby.
Nothing was ever enough. But I don't recall it
as a bad time, that November, that sad month,
kind of like each day was a bizarre vacation,
a slow parade of hours leading us toward
the hysteria of a workday, our usual lives.

DURING A LULL

Even here, on the red planet,
after the mania of moving subsided,
I found us unbearably human:

Euphemisms were inappropriate,
that now we needed to set our sights
upon some other distant orb, an

inherent hunger in us, a drive
to plant flags before the coming
of darkness. Look how we took

a barren world, vacuumed away
stone and debris, pumped in water
and breath itself, how we found life

hiding like a fugitive, flushed it out,
harnessed it, absorbed it like Rome
claiming the brides of its subjects.

And still: this anthropomorphic march,
the cosmos itself becoming a portrait
of human need. Like Erisychthon

starving in the forest, my stomach rumbles
before a full plate, slave to eternal pangs,
the space that remains unconquered.

IT IS ALREADY DECIDED

A young acolyte shaves his head,
tattoos *love* and *hate* across his knuckles.

His mother will stop eating again
three days after the war begins.

The CEO plays with an abacus.
A bulldozer strikes oil. Promises.
Someone torches the farm for nothing.

A bald man parked next to a cornfield
wrestles a child into the trunk of a Cadillac.

A traveling salesman prays. A pay phone rings,
the crazed voice on the other end shrieking,
"The new messiah was just delivered, a stillbirth."

A BAD TRIP
for Alan

We were riding along those labyrinthine dirt roads,
and I was in the smoky back of someone's souped up
Trans Am with Danielle; stoned, paranoia
spattering over me like mud, and I kept stuttering,
We're going to crash, and Danielle insisted,
No, we're not, her words throbbing in my ears,
my mind drifting in and out of my body
like a bee buzzing around a bush. I felt myself
disintegrating, rising like vapor through the roof,
and then the sky was snarling and the dirt road
was opening underneath me. I yelled, *Let me out!*
Someone said, *Man, we're in the middle of nowhere,*
but it didn't matter. I had to be alone, away from
the mouths and voices, alone to deal with the monster
dancing in my skull. The driver pulled over and I got out,
and they sped off, leaving a wake of dust, exhaust running
hot, greasy fingers all over me. I stumbled into the woods
and fell asleep, and when I woke up, the moon was full,
hanging from charcoal sky like a bulging grape. A dog
was howling. I found my way back to Route 6. By the time
the sun rose, I had made it into town, and I stopped and bought
a six-pack, drank it in a park behind the post office. That night,
Mark Settle and I totaled his new Mustang, left the car crashed
in the ditch, wheels still spinning. We ended up at a party
in Hogback County, Danielle gave me a blow-job in somebody's
parents' bedroom, and this is just how my life was for a time.

WALKING UNSURE OF MYSELF
(Election Day, 2004)

for Richard

A black dog snarls behind a white fence.

I'm changing my clothes like a good American.

A man gives birth to a war; his wife
suckles it until her breasts bleed like IV bags.

Handprints on a Christmas card.
The receiver has not been hung up.
The taxi driver keeps honking his horn.

What occurs between breaths is a red herring.

The kettle has been whistling for an hour,
and I think something is wrong downstairs.

A man is selling fake flowers outside the post office.

The fortune teller is battling a migraine.
Wind has swallowed my itinerary.

A man in blue goggles is on his knees outside the bank.
The rape victim is scrubbing herself with a steel brush.

I cannot keep my hands off the telephone.
I am married to machines, and part of me is dying.

I am in a black hole picking tomatoes.

The heiress holds her hand over a lit candle.

Someone is planning a bank robbery.
The nun is renouncing her vows.

The tycoon wants to push the prom queen onto the subway track.

Another fast-food restaurant plants its flag in our hearts.

Flies are circling the dead bird. I forgot to pick up milk.

The war is just beginning. I need to buy new shoes.

The dog in the next yard is missing an ear.
Effigies are being burned in the ball field.

I was blowing up a doll when I heard the news.

The brakes were shot, and we had to crash into the wall.

I cut down the oak as my mother wept in our doorway.

Neighbors kept coming, bringing meatloaf and deli trays.

Blood on the blackboard.
Lunchboxes scattered in the gymnasium.

We were glued to the television,
waiting for reports on the plane crash.

A snail is slithering across the interstate.
The debutante enters the unemployment office.

Take this carnation before night falls;
soon we will be too busy to talk.

There is a shotgun shell in the sandbox,
a dead cardinal on the basketball court.

Someone has left a cigarette burning on the altar.

The valedictorian plucked the wings of a butterfly.
The wrestler broke his arm doing a cartwheel.

I woke up with leaves in my hair.
There was ketchup on my diploma.

So many compulsions, so little time.

I swear I saw a woman struggling in the backseat.

It is my job to clean the dragon's teeth.

The shutters hadn't been opened for years;
light stampeded through the glass, and I recalled
collecting nets in Phoenicia. I died a violent death.

There were tire tracks on the museum floor.

So much space, so little god.

The baby was floating facedown in the swimming pool.

We walked barefoot through fields of snow.
Doves were flying above the belching chimneys.

The helicopter is on fire. The cop loads his rifle.

A robin is perched on the molester's gravestone.
There is police tape around the monkey bars.

A man in a wheelchair spins in the intersection.

A tortoise is crawling through tar.

I placed my ballot in the dead monster's mouth.

THROUGH MIST THE SIZE OF ELEPHANT TUSKS

The hermeneutical giant
plods, scrawling

commandments
in a burning margin.

The peacock
starves by torchlight.

Love is no longer
the gambler's wild card.

The jungle's face
has been shaved

like a model's armpit.
This morning three people

grieved the passing of the beast.

INSTINCTS
for Chris

I have a friend with a drunken soul,
who each day practices measured actions.

I meet him for breakfast, and we walk
under overcast skies through streets

of an exploding town. We are talking about
airplanes, and I say I love the weightless soaring,

choreography of clouds; have no fear of
the steel engine locking, the winged machine

shaking like a plastic toy in a child's hand;
dying in a conflagration of gas and fire.

Sober as I am, I say, my fear is to die on the runway.
He feels the opposite, does not want to perish in

the familiar sky, each of us hoping that in death
we will have transcended our own clinging natures,

the compulsiveness of personality, left behind a testimony–
though born of earth we died in the air, or vice versa,

concluding our journeys in forbidden places
far from where they began.

BIOGRAPHY OF A BOTTOM

At the top of the stairs in the green retro bar,

a young man juggles his mother's shadow.

A parrot is perched on a blue banister.

Tomorrow the young man will interview

a mail-order bride. He will give up on his stallions.

He will find himself in a haunted motel room

sipping a grail of hemlock. The moon simmers like pot roast.

A dominatrix reads from the Book of Job.

The young man juggles his own genitals in a dim alley

while purchasing a pistol. A boa slithers across his foot.

Someone is singing into an absinthe bottle.

The young man is doing crosswords and reading personals.

He doesn't trust clocks. His eyes are glazed like Easter ham.

He juggles towns and strangers. He spends evenings

at rural crossroads serenading his shadow, attends

coffee-shop readings dressed as Napoleon or Dali.

He burns like a taper in the face of desire's calculus.

Summer is beyond his belief, a superstition of shadows,

a fact impaled on a human rib bone. He shimmers

like oil in water. He grows wings and sheds hair.

He becomes obsessed with Pegasus, spends afternoons

researching Ovid. He draws hieroglyphics on his thighs.

He steals trophies from high school gymnasiums,

adopts Elizabethan lingo, stammers in an eagle's pose.

He traces perfect circles on sidewalks and claims to know

Beelzebub. He wears a chastity belt on Mondays and Thursdays,

sorts through mail as if it were the body of some foreign Eve.

He plumbs newspapers as if he were a plastic surgeon.

He collects disappointment. He lives with a thermometer.

He lives with a hammer. Streets knot like a Persian's hair.

His guts meander, organs as slick as candle wax. He juggles punishment.

The promised land is a dewdrop glimmering on a waxed car hood.

He chases his shadow, bemoans the jazz of divine intervention.

His muse turns to salt on a Sunday in August.

Perfume triggers flashbacks. He takes photographs

exclusively in black and white. He baptizes himself

in a city fountain while derelicts and hospital parolees

croon top-forty songs. Lampposts are possible conspirators.

He discusses the Koran with crows, carves anagrams into a fig tree.

Yellow becomes uncompromising. Impulses congeal like gravy.

He shaves himself, rents fetish movies, spends holidays alone.

Sable and mauve are the cornerstones of his philosophy.

Analysis is an old suit. He opens barnacled eyes onto postcard vistas,

panoramas as horizontal as grief. The mix of vinegar and logic.

A scrapbook. The fissure and the momentum. The jar and the open hand.

Tarot cards and matutinal celebrations. His demotion of orgasm.

He watches tomorrow die as if it were a deer hit by a car.

His emergence is as miraculous as speech, as defiant as conception.

Fragile gods, shivering in a wet wind, behold him with ribaldry.

Their arms drag the ground, atavisms starving for a human light.

BEFORE I LEAVE

Already I see myself turning into salt
at the doorway of 2006. The country
is blowing up, and the sun is yodeling,
and the air is filled with monarchs.
I am wearing red shoes, studying obituaries.
A dollar bill is floating in the toilet bowl.
Thank you for the marbles, balloons, razor wire,
dreams of mercy. The alarm has been ringing for hours.
Math remains math. I'm not sure if I'm in a signing mood.
Best of luck with your tigers, parrots, horses, serpents.
This time signature is indeed an odd one.
I'll wear a tuxedo to our next festival of mud.
Shalom. Halleluiah. May your armageddons be fruitful.

74

ACKNOWLEDGMENTS

The author wishes to thank the editors of the following publications, in which many of these poems first appeared:

Adagio Verse Quarterly: "Eulogy for My Mother," "Narcissism"
Adirondack Review: "Before I Leave"
The Drunken Boat: "Angelica Tells Her Story," "Before Anything Settles," "Breathing," "Things Are Happening Too Fast"
Full Circle: "In the Making"
Gin Bender: "The Consummation"
The Iconoclast: "Verboten"
Lily: "New York Memory #3," "New York Memory #14"
The Long Islander: "Notice"
The Magazine of Speculative Poetry: "Last Words"
Main Street Rag: "The Ascent"
Melic Review: "Biography of a Bottom"
Moonwort Review: "New York Memory #10," "Instincts"
Offcourse: "One Night in Arizona," "Walking Unsure of Myself"
Poetrybay: "Vacillations"
Poetry Niederngasse: "The Void"
Riven: "A Small Space"
Sometimes City: "What I Said to Myself"
Star*Line: "During a Lull," "In a Revolving Door"
Three Candles: "Instant Message from a Bigwig," "The Legacy," "Meanwhile"
Ur-Vox: "Fade," "Five," "In a Day's Journey"
WAH: "A Bad Trip," "So Many Lives"

"Ambivalence" first appeared in Gival Press's anthology *Poetic Voices Without Boundaries* (2005), edited by Robert Giron.

"Verboten" will appear in Time Being Books' anthology *Blood to Remember: American Poets on the Holocaust* (2007), edited by Charles Fishman.

76

ABOUT THE AUTHOR

John Amen's debut poetry collection, *Christening the Dancer*, was released by Uccelli Press in 2003 and nominated for various awards, including the Kate Tufts Award, the Lenore Marshall Award, and the Brockman-Campbell Prize. His poetry and fiction have been published in numerous magazines and journals, and he was recently nominated for a Pushcart Prize. Amen is a songwriter and musician; his first solo recording, *All I'll Never Need*, was released by Cool Midget Records in 2005. Visit the Cool Midget website at coolmidget.com for more information. He is also an artist, working primarily with acrylics on canvas. Further information is available on his personal website: johnamen.com. Amen travels widely giving readings, doing musical performances, and conducting workshops. He founded and continues to edit the award-winning literary bimonthly, *The Pedestal Magazine* (thepedestalmagazine.com).